Swirl of Emotions

CYRIL OGHOMEH

authorHOUSE®

AuthorHouse™
1663 Liberty Drive
Bloomington, IN 47403
www.authorhouse.com
Phone: 1-800-839-8640

Published by AuthorHouse 12/12/2014

ISBN: 978-1-4969-5941-6 (sc)
ISBN: 978-1-4969-5942-3 (e)

Library of Congress Control Number: 2014922337

Contents

Dedication

To my family

Acknowledgement

To my lovely wife Olayinka Oghomeh, for the sunshine you bring into my life. To my children, I draw inspiration from you all. To my family, friends and colleagues who have supported me in good measure all through the years, I say Thank You.

Introduction

At its best, if you liked my first collection of poems titled Eternal Rhapsody, you will definitely love and enjoy Swirl of Emotions. The various poems capture my understanding of what affects us as individuals, families and society at large. It goes well beyond to define human relationships, marriages, true love, heart breaks and calamities, religion, individuals, hobbies and interests, also all other social issues and ideas. Many of the poems has funny remarks, as it makes use of animal characters to convey deep emotional feelings, as depicted in such poems like the Male Argonaut and Diamond Watchman Goby, also full of information on lovely places of interest and things to do.

The more enthralled you are with my provocative innuendos such as in the Flamingo Tongue Snail, the more thrilled it eases you into more entertaining and dramatic poem like Rock Bottom. From the first poem to the last poem in the book, you are highly entertained, informed and amused by my easy to read and subtle style of writing. At every stage, there is an exchange of emotions and dialogue, as you invariably relate with the characters to your present circumstances in life.

All I See is You

I'm a lonely traveler; my books are placed on my put away table
Miles and miles away on my journey I see on the train tracks redolent
Gardenias, Dianthus, Magnolias, Lavenders and Lily-of- the- Valley flowers
The train keeps moving on, reverberating the feeling of you into my silent songs
Excited though, am trying hard to concentrate on my journey,
I see missing pairs of shoes on the road, who owns them?
I wish to sing to you about untrammeled moments like this-
Why can Swainson's thrush easily swivel in the air and sing sweet compassionate songs
How did pigeons use to do extraordinary things with transmitting messages?
    Can I have one to fly and see you with a letter when your ship leaves for Bahamas?
    The colors of chocolates can sally a woman, how come
    The taste of it smothers and relines your senses to cherish it more and want sex?
This bears witness to all that is sown into my thoughts right now
The opportunities created by this splendor are endless if you learn to swoon with it.

I want to belong to you and rehash the alluring attributes too-

I see the trees by the arbor, gold dry leaves on the ground
What makes them fall?
I see the rocks and the mountains,
Who shaped and brought them there?
Sheep's in baggy coats in farms, horses running freely
How come they are gaily dressed for all the seasons?
I won't go beyond describing what the oceans breeze is doing
to me right now, it makes me wish for you to be right here
To take off my briefs while am reminiscing, it's like an aphrodisiac.
I will limit my feelings and talk about the azure sky above
Believe me am fain, and over the vista all I see is you.

Farewell my lady, who dare says there is no excitement and sense in casting imageries on a long eventful journey.

Wishing Well

My Boo shake the coins like game dices in your ear
Heaven sees your true desire; fairies are around too to hear you
But, can two tosses into the wishing well do the magic?

Babe I'm willing to throw a million coins to conquer your affects
I am the quintessential mister sanctified in birth to love you,
And to move you over to another throne of abyss

My Boo you have hope of having me, and I hear all your silent prayers
You've conquered all the unseen gestures shown to me
by other virtuous seekers, am ready to show you my interest.
Am well endowed with many promising subtleties,
You need to have an aficionado for my many wonders.

Babe in my bid to have you, in my mind, I'm compelling the coins to drop right
The wishing well is my last commensally hope of having my wishes come true,
I have invited the heaven and other deities to come together and show me how
to conquer your affects.

Rock Bottom

I thought I'll be scared to share my dreams again with you
Your allure my lady, has no contestations!
The penchant to still dream with all the odds stacking at me is a divine courage.
What can be worst?
Am surrounded merely by eleven mortals who have heard
From me that my sheaves rose above theirs, and they have to honor me
It's my destiny to be sold far away from my kindred; will that be my rock bottom?

Unscathed, I dare to dream again of a lifetime with you.
Your star shines bright in the sky for me to follow.
My dreams will have no inhibitions tonight
Since I believe your flaming lips has been splayed and waiting for my penetration
Nothing can take charge of my reins 'cos I dream of your svelte body
Long enough to break into the somnolence of danger
My dream of you is not encased; it runs freely like wild horses in the field
Will that be my rock bottom?

What can be worst?

Stepping on a stone fish while searching for corals to adorn you with

I am unmoved by your specter character not to be seen, picked and loved again,

You can disguise what you really feel inside with your show of no interest in me

I want to tell you until I hit rock bottom the quest for you will be foremost in my mind.

Beautiful Mind

Mightily, visions I see of us is like spending eternity with you on Elysium
I have opened my thoughts to you, wide as the mountain caves in the sea
Let your eyelets peer through the open curtains and see the stage set for us
To see the sunshine outside, to see the benevolent colors of spring
To see the new petals of flowers blossoming from the redbud trees

I see the mystery that hides behind your eyes for sure.
As you sway to the rhythm of the songs strumming from the violin
Your laughter brings me joy. When you slid your hands over my chest
As your hands move swiftly inside my shirt, the quivering of my body to your touch
Makes me close my eyes gently and wonder what your love holds for me:
It could be fresh roses every morning with breakfast in bed
    Low cut plunging clothes from Vera Wang and diamonds from Cartier
    Wine tasting with you in Austria's vineyard
I know whatever I fantasize about; your beautiful mind will make happen.

Martha

My Queen, you are blooming in every way I thought you'll do
I want you to believe the unseen sensational rhythm in my heart
And call it my endearing soul songs to you.
You are defiantly provocative when you cross your lovely legs
It succinctly guards my eyes up and down your svelte body;
I lay here on my bed reminiscing you sleeping au naturel
The firmness of your breast is out rightly gorgeous
I imagine it to be the spring of your chastity
I am like an emperor penguin, the only one that can guard your abyss
I want to touch you again and again and caress your body because
I always like the romance and to feel the chagrin of your body
when I make you cum. It's an absolute peace when I embrace you to sleep
In your suave way you have assailed all my past murmurings
And replaced it with a pleasant light that touches my heart
I'm all for you Martha, if you will please hold on to my soul.

Jade

You can verify my list of attractions as treasures that I bring to you
Since you want me to show my committal to you
I will ascribe to you something I can only see in my dreams
Its perfection beyond anything I've ever seen before like a phantasm
While I sing songs of beauty to you it's possible I get
The desire to say some daring words of allurement to you
It's alright for you to join me in creating this perfect love song,
The ebbs and flow of it I can already hear in my mind.

I close my eyes and smell you like the whiff of a rich barley field
I see you repose on your terrace, with dark glasses on drinking a Pink Moscato
I spoke twice to you because your requital is much too good to be true
I will ardently seek to make you my queen in every way possible
I promise each day, my desire and need of you will increase by the moment

I close my eyes again and see the shock of your golden hairs ensemble
As you repose on your terrace, with dark glasses on drinking a Pink Moscato
I now understand your penchant for the jade loop dropping earrings you have on
I infer you want me to aspire to take on your perspective.

Promise

I promise to make you happy with me
If it was solely my decision I will make you the lambent light
That guides my wit to say the right things to you.
I now know that heavenly grace propels the witty to be quick with conviction
I now know that am divinely aided by Athena's wisdom to speak of your beauty nicely.
What if moments of my solitude are never empty but they are full of the times
I rejoice with the thoughts of caressing and kissing you?
The opulence of your style has conquered me,
Your coyness invites me to pound my chest and be chivalrous,
That's why I'll be able to handle you like a wraith.
I make my own promise to you that no matter how much more
you want to splay your dreams, I will move with you to see
and reach the edges of these splendor.
I can eagerly tell you that am heart and soul into you.

Horizon

Let there be peace in your heart 'cos I am here to stay
Nothing can take away all my praise for you
In camaraderie, I mingle with the free fireflies to create an ardor for you
I only seek your vision for us to be able to do something different together
Like roam all the steppes of this world chasing monarch butterflies
The thrill of it will inform my decision to believe in you as my soul mate
Because you alone have tasted my coyness
Check with me, you are always in my horizon
It is my request to you that you sing with intent
I am like a bird brooding over her eggs, nothing ensembles more
Than what you are offering, the ermine coats you gave to me are beautiful
I see them as your conquering effects on me.

You Are My Desire

I'll kiss you gently, and then love you as my new yellow Camaro
This will set up the magnitude for the platform I need to smolder you with.
I'll touch you lovingly, and then tell you Ja'dore
As I sing, the sequestered room I envisioned for us is ready
Am already quivering to your soft whispers only to realize it's not yet the
End of the night for you to undress and put on your sexy lacy lingerie on.
Babe, the subtleties of your wonder comes strumming in my mind as
I have to passionately go through your pristine curves carte blanche
Touching and swiftly feeling your bearded clam.
Your Cumming, pure and sensual will be like the startling sound
Of an owl flight that is heard in the dark.
The music ignites my pleasure as we dance close to each other
It gives me warmth to say you are my desire as I stare straight into your eyes.

I Seek You

So many promises like the ones I've heard you say
encompass me. Moved by your loving attributes
Am gently coming around to see your vision for us
Show me two things though-
How you will incessantly fuss on me when am in distress,
And how your love for me will be endless?

I seek you like the zest of a hummingbird beating wings to flower nectars.
Intuitively, from your amorous remarks to my sharp fitting suits
I've learnt that you need a partner with you in your suites
I've set my eyes and heart on the quest to have nothing but the best.
I can do all the immeasurable swells too like birds mating calls
It makes me reminisced the russet noise from the blanket cover over you
It's a song I hear constantly in my head, it's something that guides me to you.

It is Time

No longer will sunny days like these be unanswered
With thunderous praises of your grace
As soon as I perceive you are ready to step out on the red carpet
I'll earnestly try to bring your affection back from aestivation
It's a blessing to me for you to be physically endowed with sensuous curves
For this unforgettable sight, I've picked up so many dahlias, narcissus and palmettos
For the many attributes your bum conveys
Increasingly, through mutually caring for each other we've found the
Silver lining to our happiness
Surprisingly, I have been chivalrous; I took us out of the valley to pleasant grounds of glory, it's like walking in the clouds
I know in your heart now, you see me more than an eligible beau;
You've made me your consort.
With nothing to doubt about ourselves it is time for us to see your hair coiffed
It is time for us to move forward and build our legacy.

My Lady

You've heard the songs that I listen to
You've seen the Vermeer painting on my wall
You've witnessed the aura of Hawaii
with me like the ambience passageway of my hall
You know the foods that I like
These are myriads of things that seethe my thoughts
right when it comes to loving you as my lady
I cannot explain all the fetching things
That makes me look at your persona as beautiful
Like the Vermeer painting of the girl with a pearl earring
If my devotion tees in you, it's because I'm been helped
By Eostre for you to see dawn/light in my eyes
To also know how to pomp your prime
The zephyr wind echoes to me what I need to ascribe to you
The sun glistens on the path that leads to your coyness
The moon gives me rhapsody to lilt with every time I compare
You to my Vermeer painting of the girl with a pearl earring
I have the courage to describe the dreams I have of you and me
So let me per chance say dutifully you are my lady.

Soldier

My first thought was to say yes to everything you say to me
The idea of you and I has stirred my heart so much
That am encouraged to make a family album of us
In the beach where I swam with you, we were alone
Unashamed to show our naked bodies
But far away from me there will be many maenads around
Selling you unsuitable withal for you to cherish
No doubt my love, I'll continue to love you more each day
As you leave me with enduring hopes of seeing you again
My lover's creed to you is as follows-
Baby, am all yours if my declaration is what it takes
To keep you feeling shielded.
Blessed will I be if I make you my husband
I don't want to live one moment or life in the future without you
In it with me, we were ordained to be together forever
I know the deep thoughts of me will make you lonely,
I promise to write you missives everyday so that
You can share our stories of devotion to your friends.
When I close my eyes, I imagine the danger of you been
alone with the enduring task of staying alive for me.

You are my hero, my absolute. I want to carry all

the ethereal things I've ascribed to you in my mind to last forever

My love, please go with the conviction that am resting with all the ensembles

you left behind for me.

That's why my hopes will not be swayed one bit with modern combat

warfare tactics. I am flying with you into every battle like the radiant eagle you see

high up above in the sky. My mind is resolute upon seeing you come back alive to me.

Lady Jane

I went very far kissing you in my dreams tonight
The color and tenderness of your lips enthralled me
The taste of your lips was like nothing I have ever had before
The purity of your breath leaves an endless longing to want more of you
In my dream, I held you in my arms, looking into your shimmering eyes
Assays the truth about my love and respect for you
Holding you close to me went straight to my head
The touch and embrace of your body was by far more subtle
Than the mellifluous songs of a Goldfinch
Am enamored anytime am in your presence, it takes just the whiff
Of you to get my mind serenading all what you mean to me.
My imagination runs deep with all of my affects and emotions
stirring your way. I have joyous songs in my heart right now,
The rhythm of it draws me ever closer to you.
Lady Jane, you are the excitement of my midnight dreams.
Am making a promise to you, for every good love you show to me,
I will return it back with an increased verve 'cos I know
There is a vista for us that will lead us readily to rhapsody.

Candlelight

In as much as I lighted the candles for our evening dinner
It was meant to spur your senses for a lasting fiesta
For you to delight in me and at my words to you
I waited to see the flame rise, steadying and reposing itself
Like an ox pecker on a hippo.
My darling, my charms are still coming up
For you to see firsthand how like a neonatal
I adore you more than life itself.

Thou swell, you are my inspiration
I can't gauge all of the memories because it feels as if
The comfort of your presence is like been in heaven
My imagination stretches far pass the meadow were we picnicked yesterday
That's why it will be a fabulous idea if we resolve to have a candlelight dinner
for us to continue our pleasurable talks of living happily ever after.

Put it Together

Somebody told me how enthralling my withal was today

It caused a lilt up my spine.

Somebody spoke to me with decorum; how well he approached me

Made me to see how pure his inclination is for me.

Since I liked his ideas of us together am ready to share my interest and perspectives with him.

Somebody will make me see heaven splendors; 'cos I like

how he ascribed sweetness to my unseen inner beauty.

All of a sudden, I am twirling on how close we will be.

He listened to what my vanity wants

And if I yield my waters for him to taste its sweetness

It's because he alone knows how to sally me.

I'll Sing Hallelujah

I'm saying it right this time
My joy leads me on; my inner strength spurs me on
From my belle praises rise as the spires of Jerusalem
To the most High God

I'm saying it right this time
The blessings from up above is making me rejoice
I'll sing hallelujah to the most High God
For his grace, love and protection towards me

I'm saying it right this time
His name will be glorified in my heart and soul forever more
I'll magnify his holy name for he alone has redeemed me
And fought my seen and unseen battles for me

Let us all say it right this time
Nothing can ever compare to God's favor and comfort
He gives hope. He is a great friend. He supplies all our needs
We'll sing hallelujah because we are safe in his presence

Jesus Uplifts Me

Here I am still standing, after all that went wrong with my life
I wanted to end it all; my problems were too much to bear
I wanted to pass on quickly to the other life with a knife.
From the little knowledge of knowing the power of His words
Am glowing from the promise of knowing what the word of God
Can and will always do for me.
Am over the top with the measure of success I've received in life
Jesus took away my sadness and redeemed me with his blood
Now am running up and down my spiral staircase
Drinking vintage wines in Austria, lazing on palm beaches in Brazil
Jesus uplifts me mightily. I am rejoicing for my new love of God.

God Be With You

An ordinary rain fell today, I see everything that
Makes man tasty for the elements of matter
On the chagrin of the Lord, I reposit images that taunt us
Weakness of the flesh, stormy times of life,
heavy afflictions suffered by humans
Fear of failure, fear of thy neighbor
And the evil that men will always harbor.
In the midst of all these turmoil
God's love is effervescent and his grace
Is sufficient for all mankind to be grateful about and share.

Broken Bottles

It swells in you, all the grimes foretold you to avoid
But now you perceive to see in the bottom of the bottle
There will be many broken bottles as you move through
The various stages in life
Some you will toss off for their infidelity
Because they took advantage of you and look at you now as a clypt
Some you will accidentally drop off even as you love them,
Some you want to hold on to because of the fondness
And how they cast you as their boo on Broadway
Some will be stolen away and broken by virtue seekers
How many betrayals you will come to know remains a mystery.

Lady Marian

Is that Lady Marian coming this way in a nice coif?

I can see around her beauty her startling blue eyes

Yours was in the castle and you brought her to the forest Robin.

Mine was in a T.J maxx store and I followed her across numerous isles.

She looks graceful with her coif on, and then she looked across my way casually

My fate changed; it was delightful to see her lovely eyes.

Also, the chagrin to go after her was mixed,

I was full of somnolence, full of verve

The road to her mind aestivate me

Her character was twice the allure have ever seen before

I called her my own Lady Marian who opened the door to her chamber

To a villain in hot pursuit by Cupid's bow of arrow

Amity

Say something to me that will lilt me up
My lips are quivering; my mind is vexed by your poise
My heart is hopelessly enraged by your closeness to me.
My loin is loose and wet, ready to froth free inside of you
What more can I ask or look for
That has not already enrapt me about you?
Assuming when I moan softly then and it delights you
Would that be an extraordinary amity between us?
Only last December, I envisioned holding you too
Am laughing right now as am serving myself food from the skillet
Am astonished, I imagine you taste like my whole fish.

Tides of Rhapsody

At the beginning of yesterday, I had this wild ecstasy;
The favorite things I do with you soon swooned on me.
For that reason I made you the lambent light that guides my wits
Regere, you have the persona I like to engage to
Your ways are a blessing to me
Breathtaking feel of your curves adjures my believe that am in paradise
It contends with the unheard songs I have within-

    My darling, you will never know how deep my soul searches for an unseen kingdom palace to take you to
    It will be an everlasting joy if I can be there with you till dawn,
    Cut me a strawberry, feed me with it and you will see some of the enchanted trails of pleasure in my eyes.
    My darling, am endlessly endeared to your loving appetites
    We can both have lunch at the Twinsky restaurant
    Wholeheartedly, we will feast to the pleasures of seafood
    It's sure the design that I need for our love to bloom.

I've touched you right; we can remember to tell everybody our perspectives
My love, I will show you more other effects to make your mind skip
I will represent all your wildest dreams in trompe l'oeil
The tides of rhapsody will continue to keep your mind quivering with delight.

Share My Life

I wonder what can make our minds commingled
So that we can share one thought of rhapsody?
Seemingly I took off my glasses from my face
As if to create the notches that will lead you to my heart
I stood at a point for a brief moment, no doubt, a walk across the
sprawling mall floor lilts me up because am on my way up as if
To assail you with the belief that I want to share my life with you.
I see hope in your character and the dreams you assay me with
But, show me the strength in your aspiration to have me as your wife?

Share my life with me, and if I hold all the treasures in the world
All will be at the door to your heart, spurring you to yield
Your dreams to amble with my promises to you
I've done my searches; I've waited a long time to have you
Everything that makes sense tees with your humanity
As we grow together, you will want nothing more but to be mine.

Let's Start All Over

I was the western meadowlark that sang honeyed songs to you
I was the one you brought tulips and gardenias to
I was the one you chased across the street at the beginning
To say how enthralled I made you feel to come after me
I was the one you waited for at the Ritz Carlton restaurant
I was the one you said made you very happy.
If at all, what we agreed on isn't thrilling you anymore,
And have stifled the strides you were following to take you
To matrimonial bliss and happiness
Remember, you are a squire, my lover and my hero
We've equally ascertained that life together will be good
Ever since you've been gone, my anguished soul waits in vain for you
I don't hear the thunderous beats in my heart anymore.
My breakfasts are cold; I walk on lonely roads alone, along those paths where you made
Sweet promises to me, and my body aches so badly for your touch now.
Let's start all over, I assure you of my commitment 'cos I have sweet swirl of emotions
That will blow your mind like the beaches of Hawaii.

Fabulous

I see the sun shining radiantly on the beach water

I can equate that to the loving thoughts am having right now

I see the sands on your legs like tiny nuggets of gold

I can hear palm trees swishing me words to muse you with

I see our shadows play trickery as we try to jump on them

An array of other things builds up inside of me,

It betwixt me to say the heavy metal band is playing

Like Sand dunes. Thou swell, as I'm absorbing the panoply

I turn to your candor to give me complete satisfaction

I'll just believe that we are a fabulous couple.

Sinful Pleasure

Ever wonder why I try to make small talks with you every now and then
It relieves me to say you are in my orbit right now
Ever wonder why I try to be where you are
It's my believe that you are longing for a companion
Since the beginning of summer, I've been in sweltering heat
Thinking of you and me commingling
Seeing you in small shorts increased my verve for you
Because your leg is like a bottle of Tigre Blanc
I want to pursue you with the entire cadence available to me
Honestly, I want to get you laid.

Japanese Garahaku

See how lovingly the sun rays ambles with my brilliant thoughts of you
It's like the fondness I have for my Japanese Garahaku
Tonight, the little trepidation you hear is the subtle jolts of my affection.
Can I be real with you? I love you so much like my Japanese Garahaku.
If I can honestly say this, your allure is the reason for my requital
And this could be the only moment in my life when I can't rehash enough of my fantasies
To contend with your splendid attributes because they are so heavenly;
There is constant drumming in my heart for you
Strumming softly like the beating of a hummingbird wings
I believe I can surmount the magic of this dream and hold you as my Japanese Garahaku
As long as I can surmount the magic of this dream you will be my Japanese Garahaku.

Don’t Walk Away From Love

How strong can my inclination be towards you?

When everything that happened last night beat my loins jest.

The moment you laid by my side you took delight in my phallus

And was ready to ride me down the Danube

I made you twirl every time I gave you some more raspberries Moscato

The amaryllises in the room really enthralls you,

You continuously touch it like the joy of holding my phallus

I hope to repeat this arrangement to win you back at all cost.

Please, don’t walk away from what we have

I am contrite enough to repair my short comings to you

I have savvy details of everything that unites two hearts

How strong can I describe how you make me feel?

Your lips have this unspeakable cheer to it while we were

Sipping coconut waters taking a walk on the beach

I seek your company and want us to be together again

Plenitude of Mercy

I told you my comments for the see through dress you have on
is still tenderly brewing inside of me
My unseen thoughts say am burning inside with ecstasy
I trust my instinct also that you have sheer lavender lacey panty on
There is no right way to go about taking them off tonight and touch your cooz
However, I still don't know if I have the courage to take them off
I could only imagine seeing you naked like the playboy posters on my wall.
While you are standing there making these fantastic poses in your high heels
Babe, please show me plenitude of mercy!
Your nipples look vengefully provocative; they are ready to
be unclasped out of your bra and thrust straight into my face
It's a wonder what your minty breath will do too
It's an ecstasy I'm looking forward to taste and unravel

Magnificent Virginia

I thought I'll be scared to share my transcendent dreams with you again
Your allure my lady still has the penchant to keep giving me divine courage
Such splendor can splay my mind to make me believe that I can walk on waters like Peter.
Such tides of rhapsody can make me create for you a cellar collection full of Tigre Blanc.

Virginia, I imagine serenading you with my reverberating tenor voice
Imploring you to come to the dance floor with me
For the pursuit of happiness I will go down the valley and up the mountain with you
Every move I will make will be divinely ordained so that with more creation of mine
You will see how suited I am to be your beau
I've sustained peace within, reassuringly so because like watermelon pits
I will cover the emptiness inside of you with swells of pleasure.

Diamond Watchman Goby

Something said to me it can be done
Moved by this drift, I want to forestall your hope
That you can dance like a maiden again, and
that your heart wall will be restored with passion and romance
But why are you laughing and interrupting me?
Am already winning!
One toss of my coin into the wishing well
will do the magic. Am willing to throw
A thousand coins if that is what it takes to swirl
The waters and conquer your forlornness
Heaven see's my true desire.
I'll shake the coins like winning dices in my ear
The deities are around to hear me too.

I see, you are still laughing and interrupting me!

Okay, I've reprised my role tonight to be like a diamond watchman goby.

Everything you fear and worry about will be slithered away right now

The sadness and impure thoughts you have about finding true love

Will be made good today, am ready to take in your heart ache.

Every filthy thing that clouds your mind and presence I will aerates.

Notice how I continuously take on my obligations with sheer delight

I want to pull you close to me now and make you swoon to my rapturous whispers.

Dress Shirt

I started my morning with some adjuring hopes that
My notably crisp dress shirt could come undone
Piercing hands like scissors moving to undo the top buttons
One button came undone, it immediately stimulated me
I liked it and wished for more of his caresses;
I feigned tiredness and rested my head on his shoulder
As I had to make an excuse for his ingress into my shirt
This guy can flip me around easily now and take me on my backside.
I started moaning softly, it's a good thing if he can quickly undo
The other buttons of my crisp dress shirt and grope my breast.

Bangs

It rained so much today that I had to stay in
I'm protecting my new bangs for you to see.
My Amore, if only you were here I will have
a reason to want to make love to you
I see hope atoll the many reasons I could have
not to want you.
Do you like my bangs?
It's my new look that caters to your senses
My Amore, the sudden weather change is soughing the
Sensation that appeals to my mind, body and soul
If you like my bangs, now is the time to have me
In the Jacuzzi

I Need Thee

We were once lovers, the way you loved me
Showed swells of pleasures yet unspoken of
I felt just now how powerful vocals of yours
Still fills my heart with so much joy
If it's meant to be I'll take from the silos where I stored
My comeliness like the treasures of a beluga sturgeon
I wish you stayed when I was crying, my tears never stopped
It could have filled the turen I had set out for the fish soup
Sincerely, for this I faulted your commitment to me
From the goodness of my heart I still prayed for you
To come back to me and assail my dying dreams.
Before our time comes I need you to let me get to the threshold
of my fantasies and feel one more time my orgasm with you.
Am crazy about the tributes you pay to my clitoris
At least splurge me with the vanities you know I cherish.

Roses are red, Violets are blue

Butterflies in my stomach could only begin to mean you are
The candor that is right for summer.
Whilst it's easy to pine about your summer beauty
My gift of an outsize bouquet of red roses and blue violets
To you are equally fetching to amble with the azure sky.
You may feel it's because you are now gravid that's why am
paying special attention to you, it's more than that my love
It's equally breath taking to take a look at you and give you my all.
With you constantly in my mind, I can sing a perfect love song-

> Roses are red, violets are blue
> When I've ascribed sweetness to your persona
> I'll take a look at you and describe the colors of your heavenly beauty
> You will succumb to the red roses and blue violets I bought for you
> They are the mysteries of my affects for you.

Flamingo Tongue Snail (Why Men Turn Around)

I know a man will stare so intently at a svelte lady as she approaches him,
He will chase you with his eyes into your boudoir and never stop his endless longings.
Instinctively, he turns around when she walks pass him and gasps
To the big size and stylish movement of the lady's curves.
Intuitively, he turns around again fantasizing, wishing he could be the one loving this lady with so much butts, what kind of déjà vu this will be?

Wow, the mantle that holds this size of an ass is still too good to be true
You see them behaving badly as they try to make eye contacts as you walk on by
Some men behave too badly as you turn around from them, enwrapped with this desire
They go into deeper areas trying to encompass it all with their innate thoughts roving around you like snorkeling to get the flamingo tongue snail.

He continues to peer intently into your tight fitting clothes
To see the markings and to know the colors of your sheer panties
He is now tinkling with the idea if what you have on is an
Orange, yellow, white or pinkish panties with matching bras on
Like the brilliance of the flamingo tongue snail.

Unconsciously, he places his hands gently on your ass and grabs it
He wonders the moaning you will make while hitting at it from the back
He swears and makes a parse on the cost of seeing you naked, unashamedly boasting to his friends he will marry you this minute if you will accept his avowal
The traces of your air and attributes give a clue to the visible substances
Your bottom holds like the flaming mantle of the flamingo tongue snail.

As soon as they fathom you have nothing covering your netherings
They make calculations on the cost of having you
Gently again he demonstrates with his hands over your curves, the traces
Of your attributes give him a clue to the milieu of unseen quintet substances
Your bottom holds; the mantle of the size and shape has deceived them into wanting to pick your radiance like snorkeling for the flamingo tongue snail.

Best you've Ever Had

Time places me with you in a blue heaven

That's why am swayed by your poise to call you an ethereal

Dear heart, in as much as I exult about perfecting my obligations to you

I enjoy the commingling so much that I rehash it so many times in my dreams before coming to show you my pheasant dance.

Am in no duel with anyone when it comes to loving you right

When it comes to that special moment, I always know the point of your desires.

I take pride in leaving you breathless in the supine state that allows my tongue to explore you

The reenactment of your smiles confirms the endless strikes that I give to your flaming lips

It makes your Cuming feel like the power of the Hoover dam.

The rhythmic movements of your waist as you moan softly in my ears thrills me

You will also experience my hungry desire tasting your body dabbed with L'Oreal

See how my stares accentuates my respect for your body and all the right thoughts

that I carry within for you, I know my ariten alright, that's why am the best you've ever had.

Unspoken Candor

It might just be another verse I need to sing to you
To get you undressed and get down with me
I still have some more grande passon caviar to serve you
I give that to you anytime I want to see you undressed
While we both pretend we don't know the song is gently guiding us to each other
I feel the sensation in your body as I place my hands easily on the small of your back
From your sheer grace and estimable character the desire to have you as mine
can be easily seen by all. You are my destiny.
I determined that a long time ago when I could easily adduce from our communication
your interest and the kind of man you dream about to come into your life
I quaintly usher myself into that candor, am all yours if you can read in between the lines.

Burning

It's deep within that I carry my grief of you
It takes some surreal imaginations like the conquest of evil
by good to shut you off as closed curtains after an event.
We were once lovers, the way you loved me
Showed swells of pleasures yet unspoken of
That's why I should have stayed sassy forever in your eyes.
Am murky inside when I rehash our close contacts and outings.
Dinner nights that I dressed up for you at the olive garden
Eating mozzarella sticks, bread and lobsters on my plate
All this means nothing to you now after you had your way with me
I'm burning so much inside with grief 'cos am no longer your lady.

All of Me

It's an easy quest for me, if all I have to do is make you believe in me
My mind, body and soul loves you like the way a mother loves her child
I want to be your beau, hot like the flames of a sizzling steak at Red Lobster
I want to waltz with you so that you can see how passion burns inside of me
I promise you things like these and other subtle profusion of my love to you
will lilt up your spine, it validates all that endears me to you.
Dear heart, an army of swell thoughts keeps strumming inside of me,
it never stops, watch how I'll keep dispensing them to you.
I give you all of me, my true love plus my undying commitment to you.

Hot Pursuit

When my inkling is the reason for my coming to you
Then I can't get away from you once am in your zone,
like a Venus flytrap your charms entraps me into you.
I could swish through all the wonders in the world, searching
for an ethereal thing to compare to your beauty;
I could wade through all the colors of a novelty artist
Looking for the penchant he uses to create his masterpiece
But nothing in this search will be enough to quell your light,
Not even the effused swirl thoughts of an island breeze
'cos you have this velvety air that always surrounds you.
It makes been in your presence forever pleasurable
like the smell of the citrus scented candle in the room.
The vicissitudes of your early morning appearance is appealing
It will make nightly dreams of you to be unforgettable as it consciously
guides the way am in hot pursuit to gain your acquaintance.

Zara

When I saw you walking on the runway, strutting like a flamingo I was vanquished
I swore on my breath Zara, nothing more can be better than your persona.
When I saw you approaching me in high heels and thigh high slit clothes
I gave a gasp, even your vivacious curves still made you throve on with gait.
I need you to see how enthralled I am by your pleasing grace
The excitement of been with you is greater than my quest for your body,
'cos my spirit swoon with your character like the jasmine breeze of the night.

Zara, when we start courting, my drift is to take you unto sensuous plains above
You are my princess; your smoldering looks hold secrets like the brightly lit moon.
You are my best friend, and I long so much to be your lover.
I get aroused by seeing you reading on the chaise lounge chair; its ambience reminds
me of everything that makes me call you my morning glory.
I want to capture every fleeting words of affection as they come out of you,
I indite them for my pleasure like listening to the Superb Lyrebird.

Someday

Yesterday's nice weather was a fine gesture from Mother Nature
Today seems bellowing with mind boggling questions for me
Will I be able to hold my rein tonight when I see you coming out
in leggings that reveals your curves?
Every fleeting moment like this comes with enviable emotions
You could see all the invited guests at my party whirring
looks that reminds us of the taste of a dark coffee drink
Well you are here with me now, looking fey in red lipstick
Ambling rightly with your Christian Louboutin shoes
The music also resonates memories of you tightly over me
I know someday you will touch my nookie
It will make up for the missing times you wished
I was sipping chardonnay with you
Someday my words will be agreeable to you,
It will reach your heart like the season less carnation
that made you see me as the duce of your heart
Someday my love will be no ordinary love
I know you are ready for me to reprise my passionate
Tales and show you how I built my castle walls with
Inspirations from loving you

Dancing Queen

Am engaged to see your sweet attributes
amidst the many colorful party guests
I admire your gray Jimmy Choo shoes and tulle gown;
it ambles with the color of your eyes,
Most especially, it makes it resonates your coyness
like the lights on the party dance floor.
Even when everyone is anxious, waiting for you to dance,
the nostalgic moment is like watching
The minute hand on a clock dials to move.
The thoughts in my head now is to caress you from the top of
your head to the bottom of your feet as I lead you to the dance floor.
Your steps on the dance floor is elegantly coordinated
it's like the fleeting songs of a charming yellow canary, full of verve
You are the dancing queen; everyone can admit your presence on the dance floor
feels like the breath of heavenly imagination.

Swirl of Emotions

Am not trying to have a tiff with you over my ladies affection
Otherwise I would have been doing the same things you did that turned her emotions off
But unlike you, my endearments to her will be much more subtle
She told me my fleeting words to her were always joyous and heart throbbing
Like the paintings of the sixteenth chapel.

Unlike you, you created confusing labyrinths when she asked you for a commitment
I turned her mind around to see the Elysian Fields in my eyes
As we dined to a plate of lobster and pasta,
This is my swirl of emotions.

While you smoldered her with hazy talks of an open relationship
I can't deny I used nature's free beauty to describe my feelings of committal to her
Because her backside caters to my wandering eyes, I dare not look at another
Its perfection beyond any buttocks your hands have handled
They are like the rock arches of the Marinha beach that quells every forlorn heart.
Pardon me Sir; these are still my swirl of emotions.

From the start I told her I will be very chivalrous to defend her virtue
Time will tell if am her beau for life or it's just a temporary stint,
You want an affair that will leave her wondering just like what flurries do
The Swiss Alps atmosphere is to die for; the snow never erodes the mountain
Its forever, that's how I'll splurge her with my undying love
They are my swirl of emotions.

Without the pure chance of mating with you for life as birds do
You cut off her expectations, what do you think her mind craves for the most?
You are already showing her a mannequin you want to share your love with
I am never going to make her day dreaming showing her baubles at different stores

I have the opportunity of adjuring the flocks of birds in the sky to coordinate their move

In raging beauty like my vintage wine cellar full of enchanted bottles all arranged in unison.

These are my swirl of emotions.

I conjugate all of my mannerism, etiquette and charms for her to know this pure chance

of a relationship am offering is open to scrutiny for anyone who chooses to question the audacity

of my proposal. My inclination is not going to molt away with the seasons neither will my behavior.

My love for her is strong; I will protect and pull her out of any danger. My chivalry is

better than the strength of a Tibetan Mastiff.

I adjure you to follow along and count these swirl of emotions.

Journey to your Thighs

Today, we will finally be at the Wisconsin Dells resort
In my mind it was like forever planning this date with you
I had to wait for the end of spring and the proclivity
Of the heat to make the Sweetbay magnolia blossom
along the paths that leads to your house.
I had to wait for the heat to make you come out in small shorts
Seeing your thigh gap and smooth legs, am jostled, 'cos of my desire
all this time was to be able to journey to your thighs
Your small short will serve as my ariten tonight.

I'll take you through the path with Sweetbay magnolias
As I ardently want to journey to your thighs tonight
To start the reverie, we will be having roasted tilapias,
A bottle of white chardonnay, fresh passion fruits and tapas
The chimes of our Zalto glasses together will compel the need for us
To toast to a lasting friendship and happiness.
I swear, your small short will serve as my ariten tonight
It will surely traverse me over your smooth legs to your flaming lips.

Try To Love Again

As am trying to love all over again
I don't want your words to take me high and lead me
Through the Mosquito Pass
If your words has no foundation for my hopes to build on
Only alive for the moment but easily scorched and rolled away
Like tumbling weeds, please don't step out to ask me for a relationship
I plead with you don't briskly lead me on with alluring words of comfort
Or lead me in circles if all you want is my virtue
To conquer my affects your words should hold true promises of love
And not full of vacuous tales of romance that you don't even believe in.

The Idea of You

Unconsciously, warmth songs of forever with you spurn out of me
As I await your presence back into my arms
Behind closed doors, I keep practicing kissing and caressing you
repeatedly on my bed and building ecstasies with you
It's an everlasting splendor I see for us.
The idea of you gives me strength, the will to love you is like the
Magic of the swell of the evening moon
If I can explain my emotions to you, it will make you will realize that
The joy I hold inside about us is as beautiful as the Palawan Island.

Male Argonaut – (Maria Callas)

Until you give me a reason why you stayed away this long from me
I'll remain in solitude, waiting for my clandestine moments with you
Even while waiting, your hectocotylus that you sent to my mantle will remain attached
To my brood chamber, I hope you know it will stay with me and remain detached
From you till you die; I would have let it go back to you but I naturally retained
The best part of you because the way you paramour me still delights me.

La Divina you are about to experience the reverie that caused me to stay quiet,
I struggled to stay away because your virtue inclined my heart to speak the truth
About our relationship and how you make me feel.
Besides the beautiful nights when we had Frontera drinks at the opera house
The battle to resist kissing you outside when everyone is watching us is distressing

La Divina how can I say this to you, tell me -

What do people make of the arch on a humped whale?

Something easily carried as they take control of the ocean

We humans, see it as a heavy load that causes distress to the animal

My own pain was not visible; it was the timbre of your voice and its effects on me

Anytime I hear you sing, I find rest and consolation in your Bel canto voice

An abode from my floating palace an array of plenitude to the bosom of my wife

I've kissed you and your hands have touched my body so many times

All people wanted to talk about was the clandestine affair we are having,

That's why we were been watched, and everyone wanted to know how intimate we were

So rather than make anyone catch us caressing in the cover of the dark

You instead went away with my soul without anyone ever noticing the ornate swell in me

I was fulfilled 'cos your hectocotylus that you sent discreetly to my mantle to mate

Like a Male Argonaut was not coming back to you. You have lost it forever to me.

You are with another lover now but I have retained your hectocotylus with me.

The Eyes Are the Window to the Soul

The light in your eyes tells me I should get prepared for another valiant
Force that will rock my world tonight because the best things you've been harboring for me resides in the specter of your eyes.
I know you want me to see the splurge and the character of your eyes
That's why you are here at night so that the shimmering effect will distrain me
And seize me like the musk of a civet.
It's an enduring attribute you exult about, I would promise you one thing though
I have great expectations of how I want tonight to end.
I know your eyes can hold me for another ten thousand years with great repose
If I can gauge all the colors of your eyes and propose to you, will you marry me?

Dreaming of You

I have this to say, since you were the last person that touched my coyness
I wish you could dwell inside of me forever so that I can blossom like Aaron's rod
Quietly, I moan inside and rub my moist legs together inviting you for one more tryst.
You know I want all of you, but if you feel I cannot absorb all your inkling
Just teach me the song that makes you fain, let me learn what always lilt's up your spirit.
I promise you, by intuition the melody in your heart will come strumming in my mouth
Some refinement is all I need so that I can be the semblance of a Faberge egg.

Kiss Me Again

At about this time I told her I believe in us while we took the train ride home
Not long after that she was resting her head gently on my shoulder
Holding unto the pole with her other hand
I am amicably seeking to find a place where I can lock my lips with hers
all through the train ride to Golders Green,
I couldn't be separated from her
Because her breath was unbelievably sweet,
By an inch we allowed each other to breath
All through the train ride to Golders Green,
I questioned why she could not see the strength of my conviction.
She reenacted my soul's dream with her cheek rubbing against mine
I was ready for anything she wanted to do with me now
Her lovely smile revealed what I know she was thinking-

> One or two more kisses and I'll show you what loving you really feels like
> I'll cherish the committal your heart has given me
> It's an amazing requital since you said I can also have your soul
> I'll never fail to stand by you; I'll be faithful to be your lambent light in your darkest hours,
> I'll stand by you and give our dreams the ardor it needs like the Pamukkale springs.

Onassis – Christina

As we sail and make awkward stops and turnings on the sea
The destination in my heart would still be Venice
You will be very generous if you can sit side by side with me and drink tea
In the banquet hall of the Onassis as it sails on to Venice.
By the Steinway piano I can hear them play Carly Simon, "Nobody Does It Better".
Christina, remember things that are ethereal and beyond my imagination
Is what I've promised to pomp you with; as I sit staring straight at you
Exactly what can I ascribe the power of your grace to?
The clarity of your eyes seduces me to unfold my sweet inklings to you,
it could only mean you have belladonna in them to ignite this aura
Christina, the lights and ambience of Venice is fetching to see
By my own conviction I know how depressed you've been
Every chance at love for you is like walking on a circus tight rope
Nothing else then made it clearer for me
Moved by my instinct I made a Papier-Mache mask for you
Of a happy face that knows no sorrow for the ball tonight.

La Bamba

Mamasita I was only going to imagine this but before
I could react to how your sensuous curve shakes
The proclivity of the forbidden song came on
Look at the kind deeds fate has bestowed on me!

Mamasita it's my pleasure to see your swanky waist dance to La Bamba
I enjoy the intense movement of your body rising to the tempo
of the song like the excitement of a waterslide. Ooh la la
warmth flows inside of me; my phallus is already running wild

Mamasita as we tangle, it heightens the sensual thoughts I have within.
the swirl movements you are making is electrifying the crowd,
The current is drawing me to grope your ass like a Tiger Shark to a meal
With your movements, you daringly say to me watch my money maker.

Maya Angelou

Spirited away like a floss on a zephyr evening
My Maya is gone into the stars were only the birds she sings about
Can soar to and greet her
We your little baubles of artiste will not renege to keep on polishing the ornaments
You want us to brandish for the peerless ones to follow
You that still have the chagrin to tell the world what pain dots the mind
Of the afraid, the civil right fighters and the forlorn hearts
You that with every magic moment can utter lyrics quaint enough to calm
The ocean and the monsters In the midst of joyful celebrants of freedom
As the Cherokee Indian see the wolf bestowing colors
I see the gray colors of your hair as a binding reminder of the
Inequality, justice and freedom that plagues the mind of the oppressed
I know you tried so hard to take charge of the throes of poverty in your community
You talked about how the poor endures every night to fight starvation into another dawn
You tried to handle all in power with a jest that your songs and poetry can
Convey strong emotions and meanings that those that hold humanity
Bond may someday hear what you hear and see what you see

Festac Town

I went to the local grammar school in my neighborhood, yes I did.
With matching blue khaki shorts, white and blue polka tops with Cortina shoes
We all started early enough at the school assembly ground learning our Lord's Prayer
and nursery rhymes, trust us; we coined them into funny songs about people we like and
those that we disliked. We came all prepared from various avenues to learn the Queen's English
In Festac Town, every parent was known by their popular children's name, mostly the first born
My mother standing in the balcony sends out an alarm into the community like a cock
As she calls out my dialectical name out
It echoes around and everyone who hears it repeats it in similar fashion
Sometimes amusing, sometimes just for fun.
She wants me to come home to eat, to do my chores for the day
Or to greet my father who just got back from work
Through thick grasses at our backyards we caught grasshoppers, butterflies and lady birds

We jumped over bamboo poles, dug small holes with our hands
In the ground and threw seeds of fruits into it to play games with
We jumped around in our torn spider man shorts as we called them
It has two big or small holes at the back of it from excessive wear
Things abound around for us to play with
We called them strange names, used them for sports
We exchanged ideas on every corner of the street
Sometimes in peer groups, sometimes in groups of adults and youngsters
You always want to hang around the grownups and listen to their tales
The bigger boys could explain Chinese and Indian movies and musicals to us
We were fascinated with their stories, especially on lessons on how to approach a lady
Depicting provocative and sexual innuendos
Football Competitions here and there, winners won trophy's made of tossed
Out containers and cans flattened out by stones
Gold paper linings of cigarettes boxes were wrapped around the trophy's
Empty milk cans we used for car tires
Festac Town was a brooding ground for all the people born in the 60's and 70's
Living in Diaspora and all over the world today.

Watermelon

I've been afraid to expose my watermelon to you
I was hiding its precious tastefulness, maturing it like a bottle of wine
I disguised my fears by making you wait all this time and not coming close to you
You have shown yourself worthy 'cos you led my body from its languor
Into the burning drive and desire to grind my waist with yours.
I feel satisfied knowing that only you could unclasp my unwitting mind
To the throbbing joy I have inside of me.
Baby, when its time, take my watermelon with both hands
And let me aspire for an everlasting life with you.

Love, Honor & Obey You

Besides the glow in my eyes what else endears you to me?
There are nearly about a hundred reasons why I can't stop loving you
In fact, I went very far with deep thoughts of you this morning
There is a nearby park where we can sit and I can unfold my inklings to you
I'll pick you some tulips, palmettos and daisies that will stimulate your sense.

If you move closer you will see in my eyes the pomace that endears me to you
It's your loving character, strength, sense of humor and faith in me
I will revisit the defining moment when things about you enrapt me and made me feel so strong about us while walking down the alley holding hands together
I couldn't tell you all this when I was sitting by your side on the cushion watching TV

If you move closer to me I'll tell you one more ardent reason why I've
Promised to love, honor and obey you. The vows we agreed upon
Mi Amor, am ever thirsty for your love.

Scarf a la Creole

Am ready to briskly explain what your scarf a la creole can do to my dreams
I have relived every moment of seeing you with it a hundred times
I will gently amble your thoughts with mine to inspire me to say something
gracious about it
My mind is free with no rein to hold me back because it's an effervescent
sight to behold
It's not just your scarf a la creole that has splayed my mind
There are more unseen things that prompt you to be at the forefront of
Other interests of mine, the joy of counting them can't be vanquished
It's an ethereal thing that is stronger than any known material your mind
can fathom
As long as am sincere with my feelings, fate compels me to be committed to
Any promise of devotion I unfold unto you.

If I go back in time, your scarf a la creole comes again to my mind
I guess it's because of the way it accentuates your sensuous curves
It comes defining you as sprightly daisies that only a charismatic beau can see
It's not my desire to see that alone. Alas! I know your butt is to die for
But I don't want to miss out telling you how your scarf a la creole gracefully enlivens your spirit
Please wear your hair again in a scarf a la creole 'cos
I see riveting tales of how the two of us can beat the odds of our separate worlds.

Emotional Support

Despite the dreams I've had about us lying au naturel in bed
And singing some Barry White music to each other meant nothing to you
It is time for me to calm my verve about you and move on
The untrammeled moments we've shared on Facebook, endless morning phone
Calls, sexting, emails, secret text messages, lunch dates and tongue kissing each
Other are just about as good as it can get.
It kills me that the excitement that I provided you couldn't still get me into your pants
Thanks for sharing your thoughts with me; at least it shows I got your heart,
That I came very close to getting my sultry ambition fulfilled of banging you.

My life has known so many array of things been with you
I can't complain for your absence in my life if all you resolute upon from the start is to not share your body with me only to use me for emotional support.
What shame my loin knows now, me the best of the best debonair
The degree of my phallus strength and the juice it has carried all this time
Is proprietarily dispelling itself off day by day
It's waxing my attitude to turn towards you now and for me to look for another dear heart
I was waiting to get a fellatio I waited in vain to get my phallus inside you.

CPSIA information can be obtained at www.ICGtesting.com
Printed in the USA
LVOW11s0722301214

420805LV00007B/11/P

9 781496 959416